Everyday Strength

Everyday Strength

A Cancer Patient's Guide to Spiritual Survival

Randy Becton

Baker Books

A Division of Baker Book House Co.
Grand Rapids, Michigan 49516

Copyright © 1989 by Baker Books
a division of Baker Book House Company
P.O. Box 6287, Grand Rapids, MI 49516-6287

ISBN: 0-8010-0975-8

Sixteenth printing, July 2002

Printed in the United States of America

For current information about all releases from Baker Book House, visit our
web site:

http://www.bakerbooks.com/

Contents

Preface

Cancer patients have a deep bond between each other. It's a bond born of having faced a potent, deadly enemy. Tim Stafford writes in *Knowing the Face of God* (Zondervan, 1986) that the one who has survived suffering "embodies real hope" for other sufferers. He says those "who have suffered understand each other in a way that others who have not suffered cannot." Cancer patients often share comfort with each other. That's why I've written this devotional guide. I've been there.

For fifteen years I've sought to bring encouragement and hope to cancer patients. My passion to do this work grew out of my personal experience with my mother's fight with cancer, and then later, my own battle. I know firsthand the onslaught cancer brings on the human spirit. I know times when hope flickers like a poorly lit candle, faith wavers like an unsteady walk in pitch darkness, and feelings of abandonment flood the heart as it wonders, "Is there hope for my soul?"

We're talking *survival* here! Perhaps only those who have been there fully understand, but we're describing the critical need to strengthen emotionally and spiritually the cancer patient for the battle against the disease.

I remember a would-be comforter who came into my room in the cancer hospital with a gift book intended to encourage me: *Cancer Ward* by Solzhenitsyn. He reasoned that the Russian writer's experiences in the cancer ward would be "common ground" and perhaps nourish my spirit. I found it instead depressing.

It is my hope and prayer that the patient who reads these writings will sense a brother in these pages and will draw strength from the comfort of the Scriptures and the observations and prayers of a fellow patient. My counsel grows out of my longtime study of the Bible, much time spent in a cancer hospital, and thousands of letters from cancer patients. I pray you receive God's everyday strength for your battle. May he give you the victory.

Acknowledgments

I want to express appreciation to my wife Camilla for her constant encouragement in the preparation of this guide to spiritual survival. Through her strong faith she has made the largest contribution to my own spiritual survival throughout periods of bad health.

I am grateful to Ofelia Gonzales, who serves the sick medically as a physician's assistant and in this book serves them spiritually through her beautiful calligraphy in the prayers.

Finally, I express appreciation to God who has allowed me the privilege to know so many wonderful people whose spiritual strength in the midst of the experience of cancer has inspired me.

Introduction:
A Word as You Begin. . .

"You have cancer," my doctor told me.

I felt like you probably did: shocked, frightened at first, later quietly desperate—and only faintly hopeful. That was November 1973, only six months after my wife, Camilla, and I had shared in the joy of our third child's birth.

My cancer was a lymphoma (cancer of the lymph system) at an advanced stage. Immediately after my diagnosis, biopsy surgery was done; then I was rushed to M.D. Anderson Hospital and Tumor Clinic in Houston, Texas for further evaluation and treatment. During my weeks in the hospital, I was started on a system of chemotherapy in an attempt to stop the growth of the disease.

Since that time I have had three other surgeries, two years of chemotherapy, and dozens of clinic and laboratory visits. As I write you, I'm in a state of remission (inactivity of the disease).

Perhaps like you, I knew very little about the kind of cancer I had and knew nothing of the treatment program. I was worried and apprehensive as I faced each test, each painful treatment, and each discussion with the doctors. Looking back, though, I really appreciate the abilities and personal concern of the doctors, nurses, and other medical personnel.

Cancer is a word which carries with it enormous fears and serious questions, especially when you or one of your family faces it personally. Because of what I've been through, I have been asked to visit with cancer patients and their families as they faced their crisis. These visits have helped me a great deal, and I feel close to these people, though most are strangers. I also feel close to you as you struggle with cancer. *We're fellow strugglers!*

I don't know all that you've gone through, nor do I understand your unique situation. I've asked, "*Why?*" like you have. I've had periods of frustration, anger, even self-pity. I'm sure you understand that. Because we both have faced a common enemy, I feel that we'd probably become friends if we had even a short time together. Since it's not possible for us to be together, I want to share some observations, Scriptures, and prayers that have helped me deal with my situation.

Think with me for a moment about what cancer has done to you and me. First, it has attacked our sense of security and showed us very clearly that there are some things over which we have no control. It has seriously threatened our sense of well-being, our health, our life span, and the future of our home and family. I'll admit that there have been times when bitterness, fear, and despair have almost over-whelmed me. However cancer may have helped us accept two givens: how much we depend on other people, and the uncertainty of the length of our life. Maybe you've always recognized that your future had an element of uncertainty about it. But now we both understand that much better than most people, don't we?

If you are like me, cancer is also sharpening your focus on what is really important about life. This is a time when we may have some regrets and may possibly make some resolutions. We may promise that if our health is stabilized, we will live some areas of life differently. I have found that I have to be careful not to dwell constantly on personal regrets, nor go too far in making great resolutions, although some of each seem to be normal and probably helpful.

I know you're giving these matters some real thought, too. Maybe you feel that cancer raises more questions than any of us can answer for ourselves, much less for others. There's a lot of truth in that, but I feel that I've made some progress, and that my approach might be helpful to you. I'm sharing with you in a spirit of helpfulness. (Remember, we're in this together!)

Life for me now is very special. I consider every day a gift—a deeply appreciated gift; I want to use it fully. Orville Kelly, another cancer patient, said, "Make every day count." The day may include a period of medication, some physical discomfort, or real pain. It may be a day of doubts and anxieties, but still I'm grateful for every day that is given to me. If we can fully live one day at a time, rejecting self-pity or bitterness, we will have discovered a key to meaningful life that millions of healthy people still do not know about.

My answer to insecurity has been to find something secure even cancer cannot threaten—a Father-son relationship to God.

In my understanding, the Bible suggests that my true identity is found in accepting God's offer to be his child with all the rights and privileges that go with it. Real security for me has come from saying *yes* to God's plan for my life.

I believe that Jesus gives every willing person a *relationship* to God *that nothing can threaten*. Jesus' life on earth was painful. He understands exactly what we're going through. I'm finding through my experience that what he said about anxiety and trust, fear of the present and fear of the future, and concern about loved ones is true.

My outlook is filled with hope. I have medical hope, as I am sure you do. Tremendous advances have been made through cancer research; methods of treatment and control are constantly being improved. Many of us may successfully battle this disease—and win. Others of us may be able to be long-term survivors. Nevertheless, my deepest hope is not in research or treatment but in God. My security and confidence grow out of my being a Christian. Cancer can't threaten God's plan for his sons and daughters. This knowledge is my source of hope and peace.

Whether you're lying in a bed in the hospital or at home when you read this, I want you to know that I understand some of what is going through your mind: "Will I recover?"; "What about debts?" "What about my family?"; "Can I face the treatment tomorrow?"; "When will the pain stop?"; and many others.

My prayer for you is this:

> God, you gave my friend and me life.
> Cancer has turned our lives upside
> down. We ask you for strength to
> struggle with it physically, mentally,
> and spiritually. We ask that you care
> for our loved ones in your special way,
> and let us use this experience for
> something good in our lives. Be very
> close to us; we pray in Jesus' name. *Amen.*

Day 1

Cancer: A Formidable Enemy

Growth of abnormal cells—cells "gone berserk."

You think, "My life is over." Has anyone ever heard this diagnosis without fear, without panic?

No respecter of persons, young, old, rich, poor, all races and religions—one in four gets it.

American Cancer Society: "Cancer is a group of diseases in which there is uncontrolled growth of abnormal cells, which, if unchecked, will cause death."

How do we get it checked? Your new identity: CANCER PATIENT. Your new task: *get it under control!*

Though fear is present, you are stronger than your fear.

Your cancer is real, but you are determined to be a survivor—you are stronger than your disease.

Know your enemy—both the disease and your obstacles to recovery.

Living with Uncertainty

Mark 9:24

Immediately the boy's father exclaimed, "I do believe; help me overcome my unbelief!"

One of life's difficult assignments is living with uncertainty. To leave the future in God's hands without demanding a detailed road map requires unusual trust. I believe "faith" involves making a decision to trust God and place my future in his hand. It's acceptance of not knowing, of not being certain of everything; but of being absolutely confident of him. Doubts can exist, but they don't affect the decision to trust; they only affect my emotional capability to *feel* confident all the time.

Reflect on the great definition given by the writer of Hebrews: "Faith means being sure of what we hope for. And faith means knowing that something is real even if we do not see it" (*see* 11:1). People have always lived by faith. But we live by faith in the God who made himself known through Jesus Christ. He is a God whom we trust in the midst of life's uncertainties.

Father,
Though my moods be
Everchanging
And my eye of faith
Everwavering
I ask your help in
Remembering
That you love me steadfastly
And that you are my
Total security.

Day 2

Body and Mind

The body is invaded with disease. Think. Think. What can
the mind do to help? They are a unit, intended to work
together to build up, be whole, harmonize.

Studies at Menninger Clinic suggest that every change in
the mental and emotional state, conscious or uncon-
scious, is accompanied by an appropriate change in the
physiological state.

Human beings are whole. Body, soul, and spirit are bound
together in a unitary system.

Dr. Herbert Benson, *Beyond the Relaxation Response*,
suggests in 25 percent of illness medicine will be the
crucial factor for recovery. In 75 percent of illness "our
personal beliefs can play a major role in healing physical
ills."

Facing One Day at a Time

Matthew 6:34

Therefore do not worry about tomorrow, for tomorrow will worry about itself. Each day has enough trouble of its own.

In a recent "Peanuts" cartoon Linus says to Charlie Brown, "Life is difficult, isn't it Charlie Brown?" Charlie replies, "Yes, it is. But I've developed a new philosophy . . . I only dread one day at a time!" Jesus said tomorrow will look after itself. Each day has troubles enough of its own.

I'm slowly learning to let yesterday alone. I'm gaining understanding that anxious concern about tomorrow steals joy and satisfaction from today. Anxiety disables you and me when we dwell on what might happen beyond what is necessary for planning for the future. Usually we're focusing on some threat to our security.

A wise minister said, "God always gives us strength for one leg of the journey at a time." His love is "new every morning" so that we may daily look to him for everything we need. Tomorrow, if it comes, will appear as "today" and you may be sure God will supply each day's needs. Dr. William Osler prescribed that patients live "day-tight compartments." Why? Because God supplies our needs fully— but only one day at a time.

Father,
Make my roots deep
And my knowledge
Of your trustworthiness
Unshakable.
I travel well
In the warm sunshine.
Dear God, make me
A better rough weather traveler.

Day 3

Get a Good Health Team

To beat the disease, act decisively. Choose doctor you can trust, then trust the doctor you choose.

Check with your family physician. Ask if you need to go to a Comprehensive Cancer Center.

Ask for reading material to understand your illness. Learn about your diagnosis.

Write down your questions. Take a list when you see the doctor. Take notes. Work at building an open, honest relationship.

Consider taking a loved one or friend to "listen" with you, so you won't misunderstand what is said.

Tell your doctor you will be an active, cooperative patient toward the goal of getting well.

Assume responsibility for treatment with your doctor.

Show genuine feelings—you *are* human. Cry, be depressed, be hopeful, naive. You've never done this before. There are no expert patients.

If you can't establish a good relationship, ask for a referral.

A Way Through the Storm

Isaiah 43:1–2

*But now, this is what the L*ORD *says—he who created you, O Jacob, he who formed you, O Israel: "Fear not, for I have redeemed you; I have summoned you by name; you are mine. When you pass through the waters, I will be with you; and when you pass through the rivers, they will not sweep over you. When you walk through the fire, you will not be burned; the flames will not set you ablaze. . . ."*

God provides strength for us to weather life's storms. There is no way around the storms and their darkness; we must experience them. It helps to remember that God is in control of circumstances. He promises to be our strength in the storm.

I'm reassured in the challenge of darkness, with waves and breakers sweeping over me, that Jesus brings a calm, a "Hush, be still!" to my heart. Not only can I hold on, I can be strong in his strength.

Father,
Whether I live
Or die
I am yours.
That's security!
I pray for life
But want a heart
Intent
On being in the
Center of your will.

Day 4

Fight Enemies of the Spirit

Fear and helplessness are two big enemies of recovery.

Fear moves challenges from the realm of doable to impossible. Fear dwells on defeat, not steps to recover.

Fear is telling the heart to quit, give up, it's useless—and fear spreads despair from the brain to the body.

Helplessness is an attitude that refuses to declare that the human spirit can be stronger than disease.

All actions you take to fight cancer fight off feelings of helplessness.

When Your Heart Is Afraid

2 Timothy 1:7

For God did not give us a spirit of timidity, but a spirit of power, of love and of self-discipline.

Let's be honest: There are times when we fear. There's good news: You don't have to be afraid of being afraid. God will give the ability to handle fear. But listen carefully: you will fight this enemy again and again; the victory is not once and for all! You don't need to fear that your strength is inadequate. It is. You have his grace.

You also have brothers and sisters who are undergoing similar tests. Let their example of endurance strengthen you. Say to yourself, "I will endure, for you, God, will help me." Trust him who loves you to help you when you're afraid. You have a heavenly Father—count on him. Call on Him.

Remember that the more real God becomes to you the less afraid you will be. So read Scripture about Jesus, who puts a face on God for you.

Finally, be grateful that God is working his way in your life. These trials are evidence not of abandonment but of his confidence that this trial will produce glory to his name. You will overcome this period of fear. Be kind to yourself. Refuse Satan's temptation that you're doing poorly. In fact, you are struggling mightily. Your Father is pleased.

Father,

I'm overwhelmed.
My burden's too heavy.
Anxieties dominate.
I ask you, God, take my
Problems—replace them
With your peace.

Day 5

Learn What Survivors Believe

Survivors reject being victims.

Survivors know that healthy thinking leads to healthy bodies.

Survivors know the power of love, hope, a sense of purpose, and destiny larger than fate, and that the human spirit is incredibly resilient.

Survivors believe the tragedy is not in the circumstance but in surrendering to the circumstance.

Survivors view "positive reinforcers" as friends: inner strength, power of family solidarity, caring, presence—and negative reinforcers as enemies: self-pity, confusion, the "why" question, wounded pride, martyr feelings, negative self-image.

Survivors challenge their situation.

Survivors fight step-by-step to repattern the psyche: building a new belief in themselves and their place in the world.

Do Your Utmost from Your Side

1 Peter 1:4-5

. . . . and into an inheritance that can never perish, spoil or fade—kept in heaven for you, who through faith are shielded by God's power until the coming of the salvation that is ready to be revealed in the last time.

Often doubts and fears seep into our thinking when we're battling a difficult situation. Knowing that your faith is not the sum total of how you feel right now helps you resist fearfulness. But Oswald Chambers, who wrote *My Utmost For His Highest* adds that "moods don't go by praying, moods go by kicking."

You will cope successfully with negative thoughts when you become aggressive and speak your faith to your fears. Start with who you are. You might say: "I am God's child, so I will not allow you, Satan, to convince me that I'm forsaken, or worthless, or defeated. My God will see me through. In the name of Jesus leave me alone." Remember, as a Christian there are no hopeless situations, only those who grow hopeless *about* situations. It's not your strength that God needs. It's your willingness to use his strength.

Father,
You're the giver of days.
Grant in mercy
An extension for me.
Again I ask—Lord, may it be?
I know your power.
Stop this cancer,
If you, with your purposes
For my life,
Will to make that your pleasure.

Day 6

Yes, God Cares

Life has its sorrows—but yes, God cares when you hurt.

Many of your fellow humans are in this fight; we're fellow strugglers.

Your response to the seeming silence of God is to choose trust, based on what you know about his care. You know he shares your pain and takes the salt from your tears.

Your task is to balance the time you spend on yourself with the time you spend caring for others who hurt.

Reaffirm daily your decision to believe in a caring God.

God Does Care

Psalm 121

*I lift up my eyes to the hills—where does my help come
from? My help comes from the LORD, the Maker of heaven
and earth.*

*He will not let your foot slip—he who watches over you
will not slumber; indeed, he who watches over Israel will
neither slumber nor sleep.*

*The LORD watches over you—the LORD is your shade at
your right hand; the sun will not harm you by day, nor
the moon by night.*

*The LORD will keep you from all harm—he will watch
over your life; the LORD will watch over your coming and
going both now and forevermore.*

The times when we doubt God's love for us are painful.
Our problems become so large and serious that we wonder
whether God thinks we're important enough to "fret over."
The apostle Peter says God enjoys the times when we lay
our burdens down at his feet because he really cares. He
never goes to sleep. He's constantly watching over each one
of us. What we feel and what we need matters to him. He
cares far more for us than we do for ourselves. The psalmist
insists that "He's near to all who call upon him" (Ps. 86:5).
He enjoys "healing the brokenhearted and binding up their
wounds" (paraphrase of Isa. 30:26).

When we doubt his love we need look no further for
reassurance than into the face of Jesus and our loved ones to
see tangible evidence of God's care.

Father,
I know you love me.
Help me feel it.
Give me peaceful sleep
Tonight
Because you give
Me your Spirit
To confirm
To my spirit
That I'm yours.
Help my pillow to be trust
My cover to be the warmth
Of your love.

.

Day 7

Stay Spiritually Strong

Anchor yourself in the fact that God loves you.

Take time each day to tell yourself, "I'm a forgiven person," calming your heart from guilt and memories of past mistakes.

Ask him for recovery and trust that he hears you gladly.

Trust your future to God and hope in him for all time to come.

Remember the Christian hope is based on relationship with God as his son or daughter. Choose today to reaffirm that you are his.

Remember the miracle is in the hope, rather than the healing.

Remember, when you feel spiritually weakest, then you are strong for you rely on his strength rather than yours.

Father, Dear Father

Romans 8:14–17

. . . because those who are led by the Spirit of God are sons of God. For you did not receive a spirit that makes you a slave again to fear, but you received the Spirit of sonship. And by him we cry, "Abba, Father." The Spirit himself testifies with our spirit that we are God's children. Now if we are children, then we are heirs—heirs of God and co-heirs with Christ, if indeed we share in his sufferings in order that we may also share in his glory.

You are God's child. You can be proud of that! God sent the Spirit of his Son into your heart when you were united with him. The Spirit cries out, "Father, dear Father," an acknowledgment that you have a special relationship to God as a son or daughter. What strength this identity gives you in any dark hour. What confidence. What courage and endurance!

God will give you what he promised, because you are his child. No pain, difficulty, or sorrow can alter this unshakable relationship. Too, you can have confidence and assurance right now that you will be heard by your Father. Tell him all your concerns. "Cast all your [cares] on him." Why? Because he is your Father and "he cares for you" (1 Peter 5:7).

Father,

Fear haunts me
As an enemy.
Your perfect love
Drives my fear out.
Warm me
With your secure presence.
My security comes
In full trust
In your trustworthiness.

Day 8

Support Your Immune System— Lower Stress

Strengthen your defense network with a trusting, confident, hopeful attitude.

Lessen stress levels dramatically through exercise.

Make diet choices that support a stronger immune system.

Follow sensible spiritual advice about solving anxiety and insecure feelings.

Dealing with Your Mortality

Psalm 23:1-4

The LORD is my shepherd, I shall not be in want. He makes me lie down in green pastures, he leads me beside quiet waters, he restores my soul. He guides me in paths of righteousness for his name's sake. Even though I walk through the valley of the shadow of death, I will fear no evil, for you are with me; your rod and your staff, they comfort me.

Sickness is always a reminder that we are finite, mortal beings. However, the reminder doesn't have to produce unpleasant responses. Some deny their mortality. Believers are led to accept death's inevitability. Their hope prepares them for it.

We are better prepared if we understand our apprehensions and learn to deal with them. The first is the fear of the unknown. While it's human to cling to the familiar for security, Christians know that the only sure antidote to this fear is trust in God's loving intentions. We also fear physical decline, potential disability, and periods of pain. These are the "might happens."

Preparation for what may be is difficult. But we know we can "number our days"; that is, admit that our days have a limit. We can also "gain a heart of wisdom" (Ps. 90:12); that is, seek to know God so well that we trust the unknowns to him. Finally, we can live fully the days that ours.

Father,
Thankyou for hearing
Every time.
"Blessed be your name,
You do not turn away my prayer
And never
Your lovingkindness from me."

Day 9

You Are a
Valuable Human Being

You have God's highest esteem as a human being.

Negative thoughts about yourself should be laid aside in
favor of a proper self-assessment—your strengths are as
important as your weaknesses.

Your wrongs are easily covered by forgiveness if you
choose faith.

Be careful not to let blows to self-esteem cripple you. You
are valuable even when you feel poorly physically.

Fight off late night thoughts of condemnation, worthlessness, and worry. They are the fruits of darkness.

Practicing His Presence

Numbers 6:24–26

The Lord bless you and keep you; the Lord make his face to shine upon you and be gracious to you; the Lord turn his face toward you and give you peace.

As the Lord turns his face to shine on you receive his peace. Peace has nothing to do with absence of conflict. God's peace can be present in a firestorm and often is. Peace is a gift of God's Spirit to the heart that is in harmony with him. By continuing to confess our sins we experience cleansing—which feeds peace. By asking for his help in crisis we trust that he is in control. In trials and turmoil he assures us that he is with us—and we peacefully relax in his care.

King David slept in peace whenever he acknowledged God's ways to be his goal. David felt safe when he centered on God as his safety. Thank God today for being near you. Thank him for hearing you when you call. Commit again to seeking his will. Confess your sin. Praise him that you are his child. You will experience assurance, peace, and the certainty that he is present. Like the psalmist you'll enjoy the help of his presence.

Father,
I'm so secure
Knowing that you're always
Ready to listen
Without a moment's notice.
Not having to compete
For your ear
Nor your care
Is a constant joy.
Before a tear falls
You taste it.

Day 10

Time and You

A better day is coming for you. A day when you *will* be better. Keep this in mind.

Time is your ally, not your enemy.

You deserve to know that everything you do to get better works better if you relax and let time assist you.

There are good days and bad days. Recognize this and you'll easier take one day at a time. Especially remember that good days usually follow bad ones.

Tomorrow is always another day. You will have fresh strength, clearer perspective, more faith, and better results. Tomorrow means you will get through the night tonight.

Leaving It to God

Hebrews 5:7–9

*During the days of Jesus' life on earth, he offered up
prayers and petitions with loud cries and tears to the one
who could save him from death, and he was heard because
of his reverent submission.*

A great load was lifted from Jesus' heart during his grav-
est trial. I'm speaking of the time in Gethsemane when he
prayed to his Father, asking that the cup of suffering be
spared him. He prayed with confidence that he was being
heard by the One who dearly loved him. He asked for
exactly what he wanted. But the release—the experience of
peaceful freedom—came as a gift from God when he left it
all up to God.

Jesus had learned that he could trust the future to God.
Perhaps I will learn this lesson and be freed from the burden of anxiety about the future. Perhaps this gift of peace,
which passes human understanding, will calm my mind
and relax my body. I'm sure my Father in heaven wants to
give me his peace.

Father,
I'm consciously
Casting all
My anxiety on you
Because
You care for me.
Oh, what release!
My heart overflows
With thanksgiving.

Day 11

Rest Is Your Friend

Be comfortable with lots of rest. Often what you "need to do" is nothing but sleep and rest. Rest and sleep are gifts, not a waste of time.

Your body rebuilds when you relax: meditate and rest your thinking processes.

Refuse to be depressed because you can't accomplish a lot right now. Do what you can and feel good about it.

Balance activity and a calm spirit.

Relax. You have learned that it is a myth to think you are valuable only if you're productive.

Meditate on a favorite psalm. A precious childhood memory. Favorite smells. Let your mind run to several happy thoughts in your memory bank.

When you are able, work productively—even if for short periods. Don't get exasperated by limited energy.

Resist turning your clock around, making daytime sleep time and night your activity time.

Be calm in the great reality—your Maker is mindful of you.

Never Abandoned

Psalm 22:1–2

My God, my God, why have you forsaken me? Why are you so far from saving me, so far from the words of my groaning? O my God, I cry out by day, but you do not answer, by night, and am not silent.

"My God, my God, why have you forsaken me?" In any health crisis one can feel abandoned. In fact it's an overwhelming feeling and comes to mind often when we're lonely or our physical strength is weak. The good news is the feeling is not the reality. The writer of this psalm also wrote Psalm 117, "Praise the LORD . . . for great is his love toward us and the faithfulness of the LORD endures forever." He knows God's ever-present love and care, even when at times he doesn't feel it at all!

How crucial for me and you to tell ourselves the truth, especially when we don't feel it. In trials we face the choice Job faced. We must choose to keep believing what we know is true about our God even when it doesn't make sense and even when we don't feel it.

Then we can say with Job—"Though he slay me, yet will I hope in him" (13:15).

Father,
Depression seems to be
Like a child's toy boat –
It bobs up and down.
When depression comes
It makes me doubt myself,
Your love,
My self-worth,
Your closeness.
Help me deny the dominance
It seeks for the day.

Day 12

Make Good Decisions

Make decisions one at a time. Get advice from someone you love and trust.

Treatment can cloud your thinking, so be careful but confident.

Some decisions could well be made by family or friends. Extend trust and relax.

Don't rush—you have exactly enough time to make good decisions.

He Keeps You Going

2 Corinthians 12:8–10

Three times I pleaded with the Lord to take it away from me. But he said to me, "My grace is sufficient for you, for my power is made perfect in weakness." Therefore I will boast all the more gladly about my weaknesses, so that Christ's power may rest on me. That is why, for Christ's sake, I delight in weaknesses, in insults, in hardships, in persecutions, in difficulties. For when I am weak, then I am strong.

Jesus Christ healed while on earth and has not lost his power. He can and does heal today. Is physical healing available for all the sick? We know that not all sick people get well. Let me caution you to reject the false belief that something is lacking in your faith if longed-for healing doesn't occur. Paul lived without God's healing. God's promise of full physical well-being is part of the resurrection hope. In that day "Christ will change our lowly body to be like his glorious body" (*see* Phil. 3:21). Paul could have been delivered immediately if the Lord had willed it.

The Lord's answer to Paul brings hope to you and me. He told Paul, in effect, "I can show my power better by not removing your problem. It's better, Paul, for my purpose in your life that I show my strength in keeping you going while you endure the thorn." Paul felt blessed and used his disability for God's glory. I agree with James Packer who wrote in *Knowing God* (Intervarsity Press, 1973): "Felt weakness deepens dependence on Christ for strength each day." We lean on Christ for his strength.

Father,
Forgive me please
When I whine.
Help me concentrate
On all that I have
From your loving hand,
Not on the
Difficult circumstances
Which sometimes
Hinder me.

Day 13

Take Time to Feel Sorry

It's okay—even normal—to have "poor me" times.

Let friends and loved ones care for you in special ways. It won't harm you; rather it will help you be stronger tomorrow to fight. The truth is: sometimes you really get down.

Allow only one day in seven to feel sorry.

Follow your "sorry" day with an "another" day—a day when you reach out to another who needs your encouragement.

You prosper more by concentrating on what you have (your blessings) than by dwelling on what you do not have.

He Understands Your Loneliness

Matthew 26:36; 27:45–47

*Then Jesus went with his disciples to a place called
Gethsemane, and he said to them, "Sit here while I go over
there and pray."...*

*From the sixth hour until the ninth hour darkness came
over all the land. About the ninth hour Jesus cried out in
a loud voice, "Eloi, Eloi, lama sabachthani?"—which
means, "My God, my God, why have you forsaken me?"
When some of those standing there heard this, they said,
"He's calling Elijah."*

You who suffer from loneliness find it hard to put into
words. Often you may even hide it because you feel that no
one would understand. Jesus moves quickly to the side of
the struggler with loneliness. His solitude was com-
pounded by betrayal and abandonment by his friends. He
knew something about moments of doubt about the faithfulness of his Father.

What attitude can you bring to periods of loneliness? You
can invite the presence of Jesus. He knows your pain. You
can ask for strength for this hour of darkness. You can say
by faith, "This will pass—it is but for a while longer." You
can surely cry out from the pain of this moment. Above all
do not ignore your loneliness. Perhaps this is a time for
memory. "The Old Rugged Cross" is a good starting place.
Also, bring to it the humming of "Amazing Grace." Jesus
knew how to be lonely. You can expect him to gently teach
you.

Father,
The mind plays tricks:
Doubts attack the core
Of my belief — that
You personally love me.
Don't let these doubts linger.
I believe you, Father.
Even in this darkest hour
I believe you.

Day 14

Ask for Help

There is no need to "go it alone." Be willing to ask for help. A support system boosts wonderfully.

Use your telephone more than your TV. TV can't communicate with you in a caring way.

Push through feeling physically bad and be with people anyway. Have a friend over for coffee.

God has people who want to feel your pain and facilitate your recovery. Be willing for him to put you and them together.

An Outlook Radiant with Hope

Romans 15:13

May the God of hope fill you with all joy and peace as you trust in him, so that you may overflow with hope by the power of the Holy Spirit.

I'm proud of you for you've chosen hope over despair. You believe that a birth in a stable and a Man on a cross has forever changed your grief to joy. I agree with you. We're both learning every day to hope more in God. We are choosing to be of good cheer every day no matter what. We repeat the promise of our Lord: "be of good cheer, I have overcome the world" (John 16:33 KJV). Our hope causes us to believe he's with us in any difficult moment.

Our hope generates an irrepressible joy and a willingness to patiently wait. Our final hope provides for us our now hope. I want instant relief just as you do, but Jesus helps us have unruffled poise. For you and me it is always too soon to despair.

Father,
Help me find your
Meaning
In my suffering, and
To refuse the cup of
Bitterness.
Choosing, instead,
The joy of trust.

Day 15

Time Is on Your Side

Caution: you may miss today's joys over fears about tomorrow.

The healing process always takes time.

Making progress too slowly usually causes "blue thinking."

In faith choose to trust that God is working his will for you—in your body, your relationships, your heart.

Use any part of today to enjoy his gifts—the smile of a friend, or a beautiful view; or to give his gifts to others—a word of encouragement, a note of thanks.

If today offers two steps backward rather than one forward, don't panic. Look to tomorrow.

Holding to Hope in Adversity

Lamentations 3:22–24

Because of the Lord's *great love we are not consumed, for his compassions never fail. They are new every morning; great is your faithfulness. I say to myself, "The* Lord *is my portion; therefore I will wait for him."*

Some statements bear repetition such as, when we confess that the Lord is our sole consolation and hope we gain strength. The word *hesed* meant to believers in the Old Testament that God is gracious and that he is love. Here it's especially precious that God loves a suffering person. When circumstances are most bleak this announcement comes: "God graciously loves you."

In the darkest hour Scriptures affirm: "Great is God's faithfulness." Those who don't believe may sneer but believers find great comfort in expressing hope. When nothing looks possible, hopeful, worthwhile, or comforting we are offered hope because of our God. Our hope is new every morning because of him. We have solid confidence in him. His goodness and control of my life is reassuring.

Father,

I want to be faithful
When the night is dark
And lonely,
When the supports are sliding away
One by one,
When personal doubts
And fears seem valid.
Show me
How to cultivate faith
When, as I look above,
The sky seems to be falling.

Day 16

Sort Out Your Best Beliefs

In crisis you need your best and deepest beliefs, not someone else's well-intentioned faith.

Adversity always creates a time of reevaluation. Use this time for positive growth through reexploration.

Trust a "friend of the heart" in testing your thinking. Your honesty will be honored and protected.

You need not understand all to decide God is close at hand and that he understands.

Happy Certainty

Romans 5:1-3

Therefore, since we have been justified through faith, we have peace with God through our Lord Jesus Christ, through whom we have gained access by faith into this grace in which we now stand. And we rejoice in the hope of the glory of God. Not only so, but we also rejoice in our sufferings, because we know that suffering produces perseverance; . . . .

The minister J. B. Phillips fought mental pain all his life. He also translated the New Testament from Greek into a modern speech translation, so that everyday people in his native country, England, could understand. When you know of his tortuous struggle with depression some of his translation powerfully moves your spirit. For example:

Let us grasp the fact that we have peace with God through our Lord Jesus Christ. Through him we have confidently entered into this new relationship of grace, and here we take our stand, in happy certainty of the glorious things he has for us in the future. This doesn't mean, of course, that we have only a hope of future joys—we can be full of joy here and now even in our trials and troubles" (Rom. 5:1–3).

Father,

Remind me that in you
Is my confidence,
My hope, my future, my security.
My only guarantees come in trust.
I trust, Lord, help my distrust.

Day 17

Understand Depression

Being depressed sometimes is a natural part of being human—it happens to all of us.

Depression can be physiological as well as psychological. Ask your doctor which yours is.

When you feel like crying—cry. This is no defeat; it may well be a victory of cleansing and release.

You don't have to "fake it till you make it." Acting okay or happy isn't always healthy.

Especially watch out for blaming yourself for not "doing well with this." You must not be too hard on yourself.

Call Out: He Will Answer

Psalm 102:1–7

Hear my prayer, O LORD; let my cry for help come to you. Do not hide your face from me when I am in distress. Turn your ear to me; when I call, answer me quickly.

For my days vanish like smoke; my bones burn like glowing embers. My heart is blighted and withered like grass; I forget to eat my food. Because of my loud groaning I am reduced to skin and bones. I am like a desert owl, like an owl among the ruins. I lie awake; I have become like a bird alone on a roof.

The faith of this writer comes right to the point: We are hurting! He asks for help without apology. Our faith is healthiest when it is honest. Jesus' suffering was not optional and neither is ours. God took our suffering seriously and did something about it. God's powerful move to conquer suffering through his Son's death demonstrates that he is for us. Paul says, "If God is with us, then no one can defeat us. God let even his own Son suffer for us. God gave his Son for us all" (*see* Rom. 8:31, 32).

Whenever we cry out honestly to God about troubles, difficulties, struggles, pain, or heartache, we know that we can be completely honest—for he hears our cry and has answered!

Father,
Don't let any minutes
Of suffering
Blur my lifetime commitment
To faith.
O God, in your hand
I find nothing to fear.

Day 18

Nutrition and Getting Well

Many people will suggest that you radically change your eating habits by going to all "natural" foods. This well-meaning advice must be taken sensibly in a coordinated effort with your medical treatments.

Talk to your doctor. He is for good nutrition and believes it will contribute properly to the healing process.

Never leave conventional medical treatment to rely solely on nutritional cure. There is no reason to totally abandon science for natural foods. Patients who do well use common sense to combine medical truth with nutritional truth.

Follow American Cancer Society nutritional guidelines to increase protein intake; use sensible vitamin supplementation and balanced diets, including foods from the four major food groups.

Remember, friends mean well, but you are unusually vulnerable to suggestions because of your desire to get well. While this is natural, put all suggestions to a three-fold test:

1. Will it interfere with my course of treatment?
2. Is it sensible, affordable, and able to be used in moderation?
3. What does my doctor think about its potential for good or harm?

To the Praise of His Glory

Ephesians 1:5–8

Praise be to the God and Father of our Lord Jesus Christ, who has blessed us in the heavenly realms with every spiritual blessing in Christ. For he chose us in him before the creation of the world to be holy and blameless in his sight. In love he predestined us to be adopted as his sons through Jesus Christ, in accordance with his pleasure and will—to the praise of his glorious grace, which he has freely given us in the One he loves. In him we have redemption through his blood, the forgiveness of sins, in accordance with the riches of God's grace that he lavished on us with all wisdom and understanding.

When I consider what God has done through the loving gift of his Son, I immediately experience a rush of feelings in my heart. First, unworthiness. Then, wonder. Next comes praise. Overwhelming gratitude. Freely forgiven! A plan to adopt you and me since before the foundation of the world!

When you place your hope in Christ, you receive a life that is bonded together with Jesus. When he took your place on the cross you received the gift of a place with him in the Father's presence. It is God's gift to those who keep on believing. By his strength each day you stand in your relationship with him. Join me in saying: *praise his name!*

Father,
No day remains dark
When I remember
That in your
Trustworthy hands
My future
Is bright.

Day 19

Sensible Suggestions from Preventive Medicine

You may want to increase, through supplement or food selection, the intake of vitamins A, beta-carotene, C, E, and B^2. Consider a small supplement of selenium and zinc. Increase dietary fiber and vegetables. (Ask your doctor first about these suggestions.)

It may be wise to lower intake of saturated fats, nitrosamines, and other high cholesterol foods.

Be wary of sensational claims for "macrobiotic" foods.

Visualization techniques, "imaging" by the mind against cancer cell growth, may encourage patients who receive conventional treatment such as chemotherapy and/or radiation.

Tobacco is a known cause of cancer. Also excessive sun, certain food additives, and industrial chemicals. All should be avoided.

My Aim Is to Please Him

Matthew 4:23–24

> *Jesus went throughout Galilee, teaching in their syna-*
> *gogues, preaching the good news of the kingdom, and*
> *healing every disease and sickness among the people.*
> *News about him spread all over Syria, and people brought*
> *to him all who were ill with various diseases, those suffer-*
> *ing severe pain, the demon-possessed, the epileptics and*
> *the paralytics, and he healed them.*

The early Christians did not find chronic discomforts an
obstacle to faith in God's goodness. James Packer says in
Hot Tub Religion (Tyndale, 1987) they "accepted it
uncomplainingly as they looked forward to the health of
heaven." Perhaps we today expect modern medicine to
abolish poor health entirely. We expect too much when we
expect that.

However, to want to be restored to good health is both
normal and understandable. To ask God for the gift of
recovered health is appropriate for the person of faith. Beyond this request we ask for God to use our lives for his
glory, for we know that whether we are ill or well he may
receive glory through our surrendered lives. We have de-
cided that whether by life or death—we aim to please him.

Father,
May I approach
Each day with
Fresh understanding
Of your will
And renewed determination
To walk
With you
By faith.

Day 20

Make Your Nerves Behave

When your system has been traumatized, it's normal to have problems with restlessness and sleep.

Resist being fearful just because you're physically weak right now.

If your doctor gives you something for nervousness or to aid sleep, take it—exactly the way he prescribed it. It's strength rather than weakness to aid your health in this way.

If the fears become monsters at night, take aggressive steps to deal with anxiety.

Your nerves will behave better given time, a calm "unsurprised" approach, and faith.

Jesus Really Understands

Hebrews 4:14-16

Therefore, since we have a great high priest who has gone through the heavens, Jesus the Son of God, let us hold firmly to the faith we profess. For we do not have a high priest who is unable to sympathize with our weaknesses, but we have one who has been tempted in every way, just as we are—yet was without sin. Let us then approach the throne of grace with confidence, so that we may receive mercy and find grace to help us in our time of need.

If you want to help me in any crisis you must first seek to understand what is happening to me—from my perspective—"through my skin," so to speak. That's why Jesus is so appealing to me and to others who struggle with serious illness. He is able to understand and encourages us to be open with our feelings; whether of frustration and fear or anxiety and anger. We are encouraged to come to God, and when we come, we are assured that we will get help—the special help we need at that moment.

When my darkest days of sickness came, I was reluctant to share my deepest fears and concerns with those around me—even those dearest to me. In retrospect I believe I would have received sympathetic help. But I poured my heart out to God because I knew that he understood, wouldn't condemn me, and would supply help I desperately needed.

Father,

Like the psalmist
"Let my prayer enter into your presence:
Incline your ear to my cry."
When I pray – be there.
Let there be no kernel of doubt
That you caringly
Hear my cry.

Day 21

Keep a Diary for Yourself

You've never experienced this kind of crisis before. Your feelings about the crisis may be helped by writing them down.

Remember, your deep thoughts right now may best be written down for personal reflection. *Be slow to share your diary.*

One value of a diary is the ability it gives you to gain perspective—to seek to be honest.

Add entries to the diary when you feel like it and when not, leave it alone.

A Place to Laugh

Proverbs 17:22

A cheerful heart is good medicine, but a crushed spirit dries up the bones.

"A cheerful heart is good medicine." I'm beginning to understand the wisdom of learning to laugh. Hearts grow tired with serious and often discouraging reality. Some of my reactions as a hospital patient were humorous. When I started laughing at myself more I felt better.

Dark moments sometimes are brightened by humor. Learning to laugh, says one counselor, is a "peace-nurturing habit that helps to bring perspective." Look for the lighter side of some of the stresses facing you. Having a bit of fun with yourself may open you to new possibilities.

Father,
Help this pilgrim to
Journey each day
In joy
And anticipation
Because
I am your child.

Day 22

Where Is God When You Hurt?

This is a valid question and emotional honesty requires that it be asked.

Christian faith provides answers to the real world's hard questions, especially, "Does God care when we suffer and will he do anything about it?"

Scripture offers this claim: God is not aloof! God has joined us—become one with us—in his Son, Jesus Christ. He has hurt, bled, cried, suffered—shared all our pain— on a cross.

Scripture offers another claim: God has defeated suffering, sin, and death in Jesus Christ.

Scripture gives proof of all these claims through the resurrection of Jesus from death to life.

Jesus' promise in John 11:25, 26: "I am the resurrection and the life. He who believes in me, will live even though he dies; and whoever lives and believes in me will never die. . . " creates comfort in those who look to him.

Nothing Can Separate You

Romans 8:38–39

*For I am convinced that neither death nor life, neither
angels nor demons, neither the present nor the future, nor
any powers, neither height nor depth, nor anything else
in all creation, will be able to separate us from the love of
God that is in Christ Jesus our Lord.*

Paul's list is intentionally comprehensive. He leaves no
doubt that one certainty in life's difficulties is God's love for
you. That love has been demonstrated. When you think of
Jesus you know that love. There are many things about God
we do not know. But we do know his intentions toward us.
We know how much he values us—the extent to which he'll
go to protect us and provide for our security.

Paul wants us to know that all things change—except
God's love for us. Many events raise questions in our
minds, but never the question *Does God love me?* That has
forever been answered *yes!*

Father,
Glory, honor forever be
To the one who walked out
Of the tomb to tell us
That he controls everything,
Renders powerless every enemy,
And receives every believer.

Day 23

Killing Fear with Faith (1)

How does one go about eliminating fear with faith? One step is by shining the light of knowledge into the darkness of fear. Tell yourself the truth.

The essence of faith is being willing to depend on God rather than yourself. Every day acknowledges that you are weak but you are resting in his strength.

Practice gratitude for your salvation in Jesus when you are frightened over your physical health.

Read piece after piece of God's story (the Bible)—fill your mind with the history of God's love and goodness to counter your doubts.

Tell God in prayer that you are having trouble trusting him and he will reassure you that he accepts and loves you.

Talk with spiritual friends whose faith can feed your spirit. Trust them with your questions—God will use them to build you up.

God Can Be Trusted

Psalm 46:1–3

God is our refuge and strength, an ever present help in trouble. Therefore we will not fear, though the earth give way and the mountains fall into the heart of the sea, though its waters roar and foam and the mountains quake with their surging.

To build trust in someone requires that the one to be trusted tell the truth, do right and be fair, and be dependable or reliable. This is why our trust in God grows stronger with every experience of life. He is holy and will not lie to us. He is just and always does right. He is faithful and can always be depended upon.

God never changes in his commitment to be our help in time of trouble. Even when it seems everything is changing before our eyes, he remains a constant help. Our lives are totally dependent upon his faithfulness. The Hebrew writer urges that we cling tenaciously to our hope, "for he who promised is faithful" (10:23). Even when we waver in faith, he remains faithful to us.

Father,
Praise the God
Who raises the dead!
Your power raised Jesus
After he willingly
Experienced death for me.
His resurrection
Secures my own.
His rising allows him
To be present with me now.

Day 24

Killing Fear with Faith (2)

Use calming techniques like meditation, deep breathing exercises, positive mental imagery.

List the worst possible events on paper. Then write under the list the phrase from Psalm 23: *I will fear no evil: for thou art with me* (KJV).

Defeat fear for one period at a time. When this is done, you will know that when fear returns, you will be given strength to beat it again and again.

Work at dissipating fears a little at a time by setting up daily challenges.

Remember, "Greater is he that is in you than he that is in the world" (1 John 4:4 KJV).

We Have Full Victory

Romans 8:31–37

What, then, shall we say in response to this? If God is for us, who can be against us? He who did not spare his own Son, but gave him up for us all—how will he not also, along with him, graciously give us all things? Who will bring any charge against those whom God has chosen? It is God who justifies. Who is he that condemns? Christ Jesus, who died—more than that, who was raised to life— is at the right hand of God and is also interceding for us. Who shall separate us from the love of Christ? Shall trouble or hardship or danger or sword? As it is written: "For your sake we face death all day long; we are considered as sheep to be slaughtered." No, in all these things we are more than conquerors through him who loved us.

Our worth to God has been determined. We are worth the death of Jesus. Christ willingly gave himself to eliminate our guilt, make us right with God, and even now he often speaks favorably of us to the Father—though he is in heaven. Troubles and problems make no difference in the way he feels about us or in what he willingly does for us. The power of death to break relationships can't touch our relationship with Christ. We have been given full victory by God who displayed his love for us. Betsie ten Boom used this truth to defeat a concentration camp and urged her sister Corrie to tell others that "there is no pit so deep but that God's love is deeper still."

This good news is beyond our wildest dreams. We are provided with constant reminders of our sins, weaknesses, inconsistencies, and fickleness. We hardly trust our motives and often act selfishly. We quietly confess: *I'm not worthy of this love.* No, no doubt you and I aren't worthy, but we are loved this much. He has determined to give us the victory.

Father,
In my darkest days
I asked you to come close,
To give me your presence,
Your ear for my trouble.
O, loving Father,
You came.
How beautiful!
If the world would hear me
I'd shout triumphantly:
He came close
To me!

Day 25

Fight with All Your Mind

You can be mentally tough, refusing to think of yourself as victim, or passive, or helpless, and limited in resources. Not everyone recovers, but many who do fight hard do recover.

More studies are confirming that stress and sadness depress the immune system, while security, hope, and a strong support system have a favorable impact on the immune system.

Wellness involves far more than absence of disease. A strong identity, a knowledge of being accepted by God, and a reason for living outside of selfish pursuits—all contribute to wellness.

Regaining a sense of control is possible. Combine a fighting spirit to live with a willingness to leave it all up to God (active surrender to his will—not a depressing, fatalistic resignation).

Desire to live—for God's purposes; or be willing to die—for God's purposes.

Remember: " . . . Whether we live or die we belong to the Lord" (Rom. 14:8).

We're Fearfully and Wonderfully Made

Psalm 139:14

I praise you because I am fearfully and wonderfully made;
your works are wonderful, I know that full well.

Dr. Paul Johnson says, "Your body simply does not function well unless your soul and spirit are in a healthy, harmonious state." Dr. Johnson is a respected surgeon, cancer patient (he had colon cancer), and committed Christian. Medical literature increasingly contains articles about how important peace of mind is to successfully coping with stress and problems of the immune system. In other words, the Bible's emphasis on the "whole man" is being underscored by modern medicine: health is vitally affected by psychological and spiritual wholeness.

God designed us so that spiritual health and physical health are largely related. That's why staying spiritually strong can help your recovery. You will be greatly benefited from reading Paul Johnson's book *Spiritual Secrets to Physical Health* (Word, 1987). He develops these seven spiritual principles:

1. Understand and accept God as a God of love.
2. Deepen your personal relationship with God by daily communication.
3. Find a primary physician whom you trust.
4. Develop a truly Christian hope.
5. Make responsible lifestyle choices.
6. Make responsible diet and exercise choices.
7. Seek a spiritual renewal of your values and priorities.

Practicing these principles helps us live in the harmony God intended between body and spirit.

Father,
Help me know
That you, you alone
Are the Great Physician.
Thanks from my heart
To the Restorer of health,
My Father in heaven.

Day 26

Being in Control

All of life one has the challenge to place faith in God rather than to follow the natural desire to be in total control of life. (Total control, remember, is a total myth.) We can be "active cope-ers" while being "active hope-ers."

A good feeling about yourself and your future is not dependent on good health—for each of us will die. Security and hope for the future lies in God alone.

While you seek cure and recovery, be sure you have salvation and hope beyond this life.

When you know there are steps you can take in your health struggle, you feel empowered and more in control. That's part of a healthy, fighting spirit. It's also healthy to remember who is in ultimate control and place your deepest trust in him. You can then relax.

God Heals Today

James 5:14–15

Is any one of you sick? He should call the elders of the church to pray over him and anoint him with oil in the name of the Lord. And the prayer offered in faith will make the sick person well; the Lord will raise him up. If he has sinned, he will be forgiven.

I believe in the powerful God who answers prayer! Praying in faith to a God who cares often results in a mighty act of healing. Sometimes, as with Paul's thorn in the flesh, it does not. There is no formula, no predictability with God. We pray earnestly and expectantly. He hears. We desire what we ask of him, but we desire most his will in our lives. He may give something better than that which we request from him. We must prepare our hearts to receive what he gives.

Someone wisely said, "The miracle is in the hope, not the healing." He sought to underscore that God's deliverance through Jesus has provided our salvation. We have a living hope. For a short time we must remember that our physical body is becoming older and weaker. But like Paul, the apostle, our confidence says; "We have small troubles for awhile now, but they are helping us gain an eternal glory. That glory is much greater than our troubles" (paraphrase of 2 Cor. 4:17).

Father,

Thank you that you are
The Father to whom
Details in your children's lives
Matter.

Day 27

Take One Day at a Time

You have enough strength for one day. You can endure and cope well with today's challenges. Expect it of yourself.

Today is a clean slate. Yesterday's tough times are over and its difficulties and pleasures are over. Take a deep breath and know that you will do well today.

Leave tomorrow for a later time. Mental discipline will help you leave tomorrow's challenges for tomorrow's strength.

Nothing will happen today that God and you can't handle together. If the going gets tough he bears the load too. If it's smooth sailing enjoy the day with a smile, with him looking on.

Pursue today a fuller meaning of these words in your life: *forgiven, neighbor, family, joy, peace, love.*

Live today in the reality of the Father's good intentions toward you and remember that today is his gift.

The Resurrection Produces Courage

John 11:25–26

Jesus said to her, "I am the resurrection and the life. He who believes in me will live, even though he dies; and whoever lives and believes in me will never die. Do you believe this?

Jesus' claim to be the resurrection and the life is his gift to all who are perplexed and disheartened. The one who places faith in him will live—and no power—not even death—has any hold on him. There is no situation or circumstance that can successfully dominate the one who believes Jesus is the resurrection and the life. Resurrection is the promise that releases us to live free from the dread of our own death.

Dietrich Bonhoeffer was led from a jail cell in Germany to be hanged because he opposed the Nazi regime. His belief in Jesus led him to say: "This is the end. For me the beginning of life." He'd been released from the burden of his own death by his decision to entrust his life to Jesus.

Father,
Terminal.
That's what we all are.
Inescapable
Mystifying
Forgettable momentarily
But everpresent.
Every day must count.
Will the sum total count?
Only because
In Jesus,
Giver of eternal life,
Terminal becomes eternal!

Day 28

Stretch Your Heart
Toward Others

. . . Think too of all who suffer as if you shared their pain. (Heb. 13:3 PHILLIPS).

You are a part of others' suffering. Remember to pray for them.

A note, phone call, or visit from you could be a turning point of hope in the life of a fellow sufferer.

Mental and spiritual feelings of well-being are reinforced by compassion for others.

Sufferers are often best able to hear encouragement from someone who has been there.

Care for Others

Philippians 2:4

Each of you should look not only to your own interests,
but also to the interests of others.

"Lord, free us from self-absorption," prayed a friend of mine. Stress naturally tends to center thoughts on our survival. But what about other brothers and sisters whose needs are important? "Carry each other's burdens" is Paul's word to Christians in Galatia. Doing this helps you participate in God's work in the world: an encouraging note . . . a short phone call, showing interest . . . a gift. Whatever form it takes allows you to move out into the injuries of others to bring relief.

Who needs me today? Not a bad question for each one to ask. It seems to be a general truth that "he who refreshes others will himself be refreshed" (Prov. 11:25). I've seen a sick person serve a need resulting in an increase in that patient's sense of well-being and spiritual satisfaction.

Father,
I pray, God,
That you will give
My friend
Your presence,
Your strength.
Give the ability to trust.
When all emotions doubt.
Give my friend
That ability to hang on.
Restore health.
This I ask
For my friend
From you, my God,
If it can be your will.

Day 29

Look Up to God: A Meditative Exercise in Praise

Think of all the worlds God's hands have made. Step to the window and check the sky—is its vast blue on display? Are the stars on parade? Glance at the trees—each a different statement of excellence.

List ten names—the ones you love the most. Now read the list—these people really love you. God invented human love: marvel that it is his gift to you.

Maybe there's not a song of praise in your heart right now, but take a moment to bow your head and say, "Thank you, Lord."

Look with your mind's eye. Do you see it—yes, it's the old rugged cross where Jesus died—you see it, don't you? Now, bow again. "Thank you, thank you, Lord." If you'd like to shed a tear, it's appropriate to do so—a tear of gratitude.

Our Pride and Joy

1 Corinthians 1:30–31

It is because of him that you are in Christ Jesus, who has become for us wisdom from God—that is, our righteousness, holiness and redemption. Therefore, as it is written: "Let him who boasts boast in the Lord."

God's way of working in the world causes men to scratch their heads. Think of it. How does God solve the problem of man's rebellion and sin? What is the logic of the cross? The logic is that God conquers sin and death *from within*. He came into the world through Jesus and sacrificed himself for sinful man. That is incredible! To some it's laughable. To others it's the irresistible love of a God who bridged the unbridgeable gulf with *himself*.

The cross of Jesus represents for believers the true focus for our pride and joy. In that cross God identifies with you and for you. God went to unheard-of lengths to bring you back to himself. Remembering this when you hurt reassures your heart that he is there with you. Nothing can separate you from his participating love.

Father,

Your gifts to me
Are so numerous
That my only response
Will be a lifetime
Of praise.

Day 30

Keep Your Soul Well: A Meditative Exercise in Peace

Because of the accomplishment of Jesus Christ, say softly over and over today, "It is well with my soul."

Remember the peaceful times you walked in nature: the waterfall, the quiet walk in the wooded forest, the bird's song at sunrise—you were calm in spirit.

Remember the times when loved ones around you were laughing, enjoying being together, telling stories, visiting. Was it Christmas, or a birthday celebration? Do you recall how warm your heart felt then?

Your mind wants to turn now to troubles, times of disappointment or sadness. Say *no!* This is a time to concentrate on God's incredible goodness in your life. Return to these thoughts quickly and continue.

God has given you much through the years, hasn't he? Isn't he wonderful? And, to top it off, he's given you a Savior! Say *thank you* right now.

Whatever your "circumstance" today, the really important truth remains: It is well with your soul!

Jesus Also Suffered

1 Peter 1:19, 21

. . . but with the precious blood of Christ, a lamb without blemish or defect. . . . Through him you believe in God, who raised him from the dead and glorified him, and so your faith and hope are in God.

Sickness is at all times a uninvited and unwelcome guest. Most people who face prolonged sickness learn quickly that the battle is on several fronts: physical, mental, spiritual. They also learn humility, for they quickly realize that there are factors they can't control and that they require outside help: from God and other people. Also they find occasion to reexamine life's meaning since they've come face-to-face with life's limitations. Often there is, as Tim Stafford writes, "a terrible stripping of all dignity and capacity and status, a terrible caldron of suffering for many" (*Knowing the Grace of God*, Zondervan, 1986).

In this most difficult hour we can draw strength from Jesus, a fellow sufferer, and we can be "conscious of God" as we endure this difficult period.

Father,

May my deepest desire

Be

To daily conform my life

To

Your revealed will.

Day 31

Talk to Your Loved Ones

Your family is your God-given life support system. You can trust them with facts about your illness.

Families tend to worry less when communication remains open and honest.

Close friends very much want to "connect up" with you. They would also like to do something specific for you. Let them.

Remember, it's okay to laugh and to cry with loved ones. Your feelings are safe.

You need each other now so that neither you nor they bear your hopes or fears alone.

A Christian psychiatrist counsels: "You are God's gifts to each other for the living of these days."

Grace . . . Be with You All

Romans 16:20

The God of peace will soon crush Satan under your feet.
The grace of our Lord Jesus be with you.

These words are found at the end of Paul's letters to churches. What do they mean? Grace has appeared to us through our Lord Jesus. It is God coming near us to help us: first to free us from the prison of our sins, then to receive us as friends, now to strengthen us in time of trial.

Grace is the good news that we have nothing now to fear. Grace is acceptance—he loves us just as we are. Grace says, "You're not good enough, but you're welcome in heaven." Grace is the reason you can be sick yet radiant in faith.

Father,
The day of my salvation, my God,
The day one life became whole
Is the day from which
All new days
Take their joy and purpose.

Day 32

Your Minister's Role

You are certain that disease cannot separate you from the love of God. Allow your minister and church friends to reinforce your faith.

Misinformation about the disease and its treatment may be present among those interested in you. Your minister can serve as an ally in helpful communication.

Remember, ministers are real people who become afraid, anxious, uncertain, irritable, angry, and depressed—just as you may be.

Seek the opportunity to talk with this fellow believer about your "one great dread"—leaving those you love.

Celebrate the release that comes when Christians "carry each other's burdens" (Gal. 6:2). Together work to nurture hope and faith.

Jesus Is Our Ever-Present Friend

John 15:13

"Greater love has no one than this, that he lay down his life for his friends."

Notice the aspects of friendship that Jesus demonstrated to his disciples and offers singularly to each Christian today. First, and supremely, he laid down his life for his friends. "There is no greater love than this." God's offer of reconciliation through Christ changes us from enemies into friends—all as a result of the reconciling work of Jesus' death. Jesus' friendship was vulnerable in that he offered himself first.

Robert Bridges observes that "friendship is in loving rather than being loved." Robert South said, "a friend will be sure to act the part of an advocate before he will assume that of a judge." He pinpoints the modern awareness that a friend actively pursues your best interest rather than withholding warmth and presence while he judges your worthiness.

Jesus created the basis for our friendship with God in the cross. In anticipation of God's redemptive plans being fulfilled, he announced the offer of friendship to his disciples as he neared the event that would make it possible. Thank God that Jesus is our ever-present friend.

Father,
May my mind fathom
More of your depth
Of love for me,
So that my life may
In these trying days
Demonstrate the
Gratitude of redemption.

Day 33

Fighting Mental Fatigue

You are being given strength for today. Discipline your mind when you start to dwell on this "week" or this "month." "Each day has enough troubles of its own," said the One who supplies today's strength.

Be creative with routines. Introduce new colors or new patterns of doing daily chores. Listen to a new radio station. Look through a new magazine. Small changes lift you out of the ruts that tire your spirit.

Have a talk with yourself. There is benefit in an occasional "self-chewing-out." Ask for a "pep" talk from a nurse, doctor, or friend.

Send someone a gift. Show gratitude. When you do some "deed therapy," you feel refreshed and alive.

Designate a set time—two hours—for the blahs. At the end of the period, send out for ice cream and celebrate "the end of the blahs" for today.

Ask God for endurance and the ability to "hang in there." He will answer with strength for today.

A Promise for a Troubled Spirit

Isaiah 41:10

So do not fear, for I am with you; do not be dismayed, for I am your God. I will strengthen you and help you; I will uphold you with my righteous right hand.

In facing fear with faith I am probably helped most by refreshing my memory of God's promises. It is here that I can find peace, a calm place where "aloneness" no longer means loneliness because God is present.

I find myself needing to repeat over and over again God's words: "I will never leave thee, nor forsake thee" (Heb. 13:5 KJV).

These words comforted early Christians in every adversity. They boldly said: "The Lord is my helper, and I will not fear what man shall do unto me." The inner voices of doubt and fear can be answered by repeating God's continual promise.

Isaiah was secure in God's promises when he said to God: "You will keep in perfect peace him whose mind is steadfast, because he trusts in you" (26:3).

Father,
When the humans
Have carried the body
To its earthen place,
Mourning has grip on hearts.
At that time
Help human grief to be transient
As one whispers to another
"But remember...he arose!"
The last word is
Life
Not death.
Praise your name!

Dealing with Depression in Illness

"It's not easy being sick." Speaking from personal experience, "It is very hard."

Illness, whether it is temporary, chronic, or lifethreatening, is often accompanied by depression. To cope we must wage war on two fronts (depression and illness) at a time when we are in a weak and vulnerable position. As a cancer patient and a counselor to cancer patients, I have found it very important to first try to understand depression and then to find "coping mechanisms" to help deal with it.

Everyone becomes depressed at one time or another. Who doesn't remember feeling low, either hopeless or helpless occasionally? Sometimes, a major negative event can make one anxious or on the verge of tears. One study (Howard Bereavement Study, 1986) estimates that in our country, at any given time, as many as 15 million people are depressed. The word *depression* is used to describe a wide spectrum of behavior—from a slight feeling of "being down" (which may last only an hour or two), all the way to severe depression. What worries us, however, is not brief periods of feeling blue or melancholy. We become concerned when we suffer the emotional pain of a continuing downness. No amount of encouragement or activity seems to lift our spirit.

As mentioned earlier, in 1973 I was diagnosed with lymphoma, a cancer of the lymphatic system. After the diagnosis, I was flown to M.D. Anderson Cancer Hospital at Houston for immediate evaluation. There I began chemotherapy to fight the disease. After the initial shock of the horrible diagnosis, I became depressed. No amount of loving concern, positive talk, or kindness could lift me out of my despair. I experienced for the first time great loneliness and a sense of hopelessness. I found myself weeping often and was very anxious. One day my physician, Dr. Francisco Gonzales, took my wife outside my room and explained. Understandably, my outlook was poor. He then added that he doubted I would feel much better mentally until I improved physically.

This "chemical depression" was then explained to me. If I understand what he said it was basically this: my body was chemically unbalanced *because* of the illness and therefore caused me to be depressed. Pep talks weren't likely to help much until the medicine worked against my disease. This explanation helped me understand the nature of this depression and relieved me from feeling guilty about not being able to control the depression.

From that moment I have thought that many sick people would profit from having a better understanding of depression, especially the more serious or clinical depression that is so often present in chronic or serious illness. Understanding can become an effective weapon in our struggle. I've worked with doctors and I want to share what I've learned about the two main kinds of depression: chemical depression and psychological depression.

Chemical Depression— What Is Happening in Your Body?

Since chemical depression was first explained to me, I have learned that although a serious or chronic illness makes us particularly vulnerable, the chemical imbalance that causes depression may occur in a variety of ways. The following are a few of the known and suspected causes of this complicated type of depression.

Most doctors believe that there is an inner relationship between depression and altered levels of chemicals that affect the brain, such as norepinephine, and an endocrine disturbance. Viral illnesses and endocrine disorders can cause depression. Electrolyte disturbances, such as an upset in the levels of sodium and potassium in the body, are also indicted as causes of depression. Hypothyroidism, hypoglycemia, and even fatigue can produce this type of depression. Some medications have also been linked to it.

It is important that we identify the symptoms of chemical depression. There are five major kinds: *sad affect, painful thinking, physical symptoms, anxiety,* and *delusional thinking.* Let me explain these one at a time. They may affect either men or women, of course.

One major symptom of depression is *basic sadness.* A person may want to cry or actually weep often. His or her face looks downcast. There is little care for appearance, perhaps not "feeling like" shaving, putting on makeup. There seems to be no point in the effort; there is no purpose.

Another symptom is *emotional pain.* The prolonged pain a person may feel is like having a broken heart. Self-criticism surfaces along with feeling terrible about past mistakes, yet not being able to let go of them. Constant worry and feeling unimportant leads to thinking and talking to others in terms of worthlessness, even hopelessness. Often a depressed person thinks, "I'll never get better." There is great loneliness. Low energy and sometimes a poor memory and lack of concentration plague the sufferer. Decision making becomes very difficult.

A third symptom of chemical depression is *physical.* This is important to understand, for research shows that biochemical changes take place in the brain and drastically affect the human nervous system during chemical depression. Depressed persons may suffer tension headaches or stomach disorders. Sleep and appetite can be upset. They may wake up earlier than usual, have trouble falling asleep, or sleep too much. They may eat too much or too little. Sexual interest often falls off. Shortness of breath, slower body movements, a more rapid heartbeat, or unusual skin sensations may occur. Any of these symptoms may scare sufferers and make them think they are going crazy.

A fourth major symptom is *anxiety* or *a tendency to be quickly angry.* A tenseness or "antsiness" can be present. This symptom can range from simple restlessness or impatience to a severe anxiety accompanied by unexplainable fear or panic.

Finally, a symptom which can occur is *delusional thinking.* The person can get out of touch with reality. Hearing voices or seeing things that aren't there is clearly evidence of a chemical depression.

Chemical depression is not caused solely by illness. Any shock or major life change may trigger physical responses that can lead to serious depression. We may find it difficult to understand how the death of a loved one, a divorce, or the physical displacement that occurs when we move to a new city can result in a physically caused depression. We do not connect the life change to the depression. However, those in the medical field are aware of these causes as well as others I've mentioned.

The many causes make it imperative that you and I talk to our doctors about any prolonged periods of depression. It is very important that a person relate well to the doctor to understand the problem and get effective treatment.

There is encouraging news for those who find they are suffering from chemical depression. There are several classes of medications that fight depression. One example of these is the tricyclic antidepressants such as Tofranil, Elavil and Sinequan. These are being effectively prescribed by physicians who see patients plagued by depression. Doctors who work in this field tell me that we don't know exactly how these medications work.

I want to emphasize again that your doctor is your best friend in this battle. Rather than ridiculing you, he or she will seek to understand. A good supply of medicines that are not addictive and have been shown to be quite effective as reinforcement are currently available and should be used until your chemical system once again begins to function properly.

Psychological Depression—
What's Happening in Your Mind?

I want to move from talking about clinical or physical depression to the psychological depression or simply the depressed spirit. My purpose, again, is to help the person to understand depression and to learn successful ways of coping with it.

In seeking to understand, let's look at the aspects of depression in illness that may not be related to chemical or physical depression, but still result in a depressed spirit. We need to better understand what chronic or life-threatening illness does to us. In reality there is much to challenge our spirit.

First, and most important—illness brings the question of *limits* to us. We no longer enjoy good health. Our freedom is limited. When we go from being in good health to experiencing impaired or poor health we experience a major life change. It's true, as one television commercial suggested, "When you have your health, you have just about everything." Put another way, "From good health springs most of life's good opportunities and enjoyments."

Another aspect of illness is *pain*. The millions who suffer from arthritis can attest to the real difficulties of dealing with chronic pain when doing such basic tasks as rising from the bed or walking to the car. When today's basic tasks are performed in discomfort or physical pain, our psychological outlook may be negatively affected.

Another hidden assault of serious illness is our *inability to control* our own future. The strong-willed person will often find this the hardest to live with. The illness will have its way and we, in spite of our will, are many times helpless.

Prolonged illness is discouraging. Illness, without question, presents major hurdles to developing or keeping a positive mental outlook. We acknowledge that a disciplined mind is essential if we are to succeed. I want to be vulnerable and share with you the principles which have helped me deal with depression during my illness.

First, I've learned to *concentrate on what I can do and not on all the things I can't do.* Since illness brings limits and has taken me out of the usual flow of my life's activities, I fight back by making a decision to fight against self-pity. I have dealt with many sick people by correspondence through the last thirteen years, and I've found that some allow their limitations to bury them. Others find within their limits the power to create life, to love, and to serve. The difference isn't really the illness but the decision of the will. People who overcome (I call them victors) have a plan of action within their limits. People who give in (I call them victims) usually concentrate on the past and on the present difficulties and limitations of their illness. They tend to live with their "regrets" and their "wishes," and neither gives them much quality or purpose in living.

Second, I've learned to *define my life's meaning in terms that do not require good or perfect health.* Often illness gives an opportunity to believe we're just not worth much anymore. "I'm no good to myself or anybody else" has often been said.

When self-esteem and self-worth are weak, it is because we have defined our lives in terms of our roles or functions rather than in terms of the inherent worth God has given us. Perhaps illness can be the occasion to finally break out of this delusion that "we are what we do" and move toward the understanding that we are the object of God's love in Christ.

One common feeling in depression is that of having lost one's faith. A person may have no sense of the presence of God in his life. This person needs to tell a trusted friend the depths of his or her religious despair. Often such persons also feel guilt for some real or imagined misdeed and may feel, because they are sick, that they have few opportunities to do better. The future for them does not look bright. The best days seem to be behind. Among the things we need to hear is that God loves and forgives.

In this period of poor health let me suggest that *you ask God in prayer for the strength to endure.* But, along with enduring, ask him to teach you. *Decide that your illness has meaning and pursue that meaning.* More benefits come from looking for meaning than ever come from looking for causes or from continuing to wonder, "Why me?"

You have one advantage (and maybe more) over most people: you know the important truth about how fragile human life is. This knowledge may not be pleasant, but it is profitable because you can decide how to live meaningfully. Your anger and disappointment are normal. *Vent your feelings and you will cope better.* Then you will be prepared to work your plan of action with some inner peace and satisfaction.

Finally, *don't go it alone.* I learned that I needed a support system of family and friends. For you it may be a niece or neighbor. But let others help you. It's time you learned to receive as well as give. I encourage you to *change "I can't" to "I will," taking personal responsibility for the quality of your life even in illness.* Now I'm asking you not to try to do it all by yourself. Just as you need to move "outside yourself" by doing something *for* somebody (even though you're not in good health), you also should become gracious in receiving. You can bless others by serving them and by letting them serve you.

I treasure the word *hope.* In the midst of the depression of illness the word *hope* is rarely mentioned. I'm asking you to consider using that word again. Hope can mean endurance and perseverance. Hope can mean a new way of seeing your present circumstances. Hope can mean God has more in store for you. Believe with me that "where there's life, there's hope." In the midst of illness it may take special eyes to see it, but the good news is that you can have the gift of special eyes.

Conclusion

You Can Be Well . . . Even While You're Ill

Let me tell you about two people.

One is a person I know who is living with cancer. This person lives day-by-day, lovingly and purposefully. She lives on a high spiritual plane, thankful for the source of every gift she receives. Life is not a bowl of sour lemons. Life is God's gift. This person has wellness. But she doesn't have health.

Then I know of another person. He performed in the 1984 Olympics, but he was constantly arguing with his coach and constantly seeking self-service and glory for himself. He wanted the newspaper interview. He wanted the prominence. He was on a trip all for himself. He had no particular life purpose except to be strong—to win. And after the Olympics, he was unhappy. He had given little thought to anything other than the short-term goal of winning. Now, this person has health. But he is not "well" at all.

The concept of "wellness" is popular today. Wellness clinics are springing up all over the country. These clinics use methods of preventive medicine and counseling in areas such as stress management and nutritional needs. The rising popularity of these methods comes in the wake of the health and fitness craze and tells us that people are seeking something more. We now know that happiness and fulfillment don't automatically come with jogging each morning at daybreak. People want to enjoy *complete* health, though they often fail to understand what makes a person healthy.

155

The weakness in the methods being used by clinics and counseling services lies in the fact that they do not go far enough. One area is not being considered—the area of the spirit. When the spiritual part of man is left out, total solutions are not possible.

However one study conducted by the Medical College of Wisconsin has gone this one step further. Dr. John Pilch and others are doing research that asks, "What makes us most healthy—not only in body, but also in soul and spirit?" Research concludes that five key ingredients contribute to *wellness*.

This so called new concept of wellness is merely a revival of the concept of wellness proposed by Jesus in his life and teachings. These five components are easily met by the person who bases his or her life on the teaching of Jesus:

A person is well who knows the purpose and the meaning of life. Christians know the meaning and purpose of life. Knowing that God is their Father, they know they are here to live in a way that glorifies him. Their destiny is to be with the Father.

Another ingredient identified by the Wisconsin doctors is that *well people know that life's authentic, satisfying, fulfilling joys and pleasures* don't *come* from satisfying themselves, but *from living for a higher purpose and for a higher power.* As Christians, we know that we have been bought with a price. We are not our own. We know Christ died so that all who live might no longer live for themselves, but might live for him who died for us. We understand that real pleasure is found in living out Jesus' teaching that it is far more blessed to give than to receive. The way of the Lord Jesus Christ creates a deep inner sense of peace, purpose, and joy.

Still another ingredient—*people who are well have found an appropriate source of motivation.* For Christians motivation isn't just in giving so that they can receive. Motivation is giving out of gratitude to the God who gave us life. People who turn from self-service to serving God experience profound change. Having turned their lives toward God they are being "conformed to the image of his Son" (Rom. 8:29 KJV).

Finally, there is in *wellness the idea that a person who is well understands that health is far more than physical well-being.* Paul taught, "Though the outer man is wasting away, the inner man is being renewed day by day" (*see* 2 Cor. 4:16). These momentary afflictions don't control our lives because we belong to the One who created us, and the One who guides and controls all—the sovereign Lord of the universe.

These ingredients that Dr. Pilch and his colleagues have identified as components of wellness only reflect what Jesus said. He came to people who are sick—you and me—and made us well by forgiving our sins.

Therefore wellness—a properly integrated life of wholeness—is God's gift through Jesus Christ. One may be ravaged by illness or tormented by chronic poor health. However when one's life is centered in Christ, he or she is spiritually in excellent health. What encouragement! What good news!

Everyone who truly gets well, gets well through Jesus Christ!